THE IMMIGRANT WAY TO WEALTH

Financial Principles for a First-Generation Immigrant

E.K. Nassirim

Printed in the United States of America
First Printing, 2020
ISBN-10: 0998463256
ISBN-13: 978-0998463254

Qomlavy Publishing - (May 8, 2020)
A Qomlavy Networks Company
200 Umber ST NW
Palm Bay, FL 32907
 +1-(321) 549-0886
www.qomlavy.com

Cover Design: Qomlavy Agency
Creative Consultant: Jim Villaflores
Editing: Nicole Lyte, LEHL
Dion St. Hilaire
Jenni Patel

DEDICATION

To My Father Komlaga Seenam Anani D. who sacrificed everything to send me to a foreign land, believed in me, but died before all the things he believed about me came to be. Victory is sour when your number one cheerleader is not around to lift the trophy with you.

To my Mother Kafui Awovi Jeanette for showing how a child born in place where most women were not allowed to go to school or those who did dropped out early, could grow to be not only a PhD but be elected to Congress and change the laws of the country to give women more freedom in society than the freedom she had growing up... and thanks for the Green Card ☺

To my Sister Amivi Emefa for bearing with me all the years we were trying to figure out our way through life away from family in a foreign land which at times could be unforgiving. I am very proud of the woman you have become and of all your successes.

CONTENTS

ACKNOWLEDGMENTS

To all who contributed to my edification in life and to this book, thank you. I have been made better because of you all, and my journey in this country would not have been the same without each and every one of you. The winds of my gratitude will forever blow on the hills of your generosity and support.

Dion St. Hilaire … Thank you!

WELCOME TO AMERICA!

During the coronavirus (COVID-19) pandemic of 2020, I found myself contemplating my life's journey. Things were dire around me, and I was praying for other people's safety and hoping for the time to pass so we could all see each other again. While being quarantined, I started to reflect on the fact I did not have any debts, the fact that I had a year's worth of savings ready for the eventuality of losing my job, the fact that I was living on less than half of my current income, so that even as the company I worked for significantly cut salaries and benefits, my living situation was not dramatically affected. As I pondered how I got here, I was humbled by all of the people who embraced me in this foreign land, offered me opportunities, guided me and taught me so many valuable lessons that my life in America was made better because of it.

Many of my friends who shared these principles were all doing as well - if not better - than I was. As we mulled over the mistakes we made and how much better off we would have been had we learned these lessons earlier, the sentence "I wish someone told me when I first got here..." came up over and over again in these conversations.

I indeed wish someone had told me when I first got here to do things a certain way, and to avoid other things. I often pondered what I would do if I were ever handed a time machine. If I could go back and change something, what would it be? I used to come up with different scenarios, but being quarantined and spending a lot of time by myself has made the vision clearer.

My eighteen-year-old self landed at JFK on December 26th, 2001. I barely spoke English. With two American Express traveler's cheques in my possession, I was scared but excited to take on this new journey. I cleared immigration and went to the bathroom. As I walked out of the bathroom to make my connecting flight to Florida, the realization of being alone in a foreign land where I knew no one dawned on me. "The World's Greatest" - the soundtrack to the Muhammad Ali biopic - played on the speakers. There was a smell of fresh bagels in the air, and all around me the crowd was moving like a never-ending stream of shadows. This is the moment I would travel back in time to. I would go back to my younger self, tap him on the shoulder, and with a big smile I would tell him: "welcome to America. Everything is going to be all right. Here are the fundamentals which you need to know. The rest you will figure it out. Be blessed. See you in twenty years."

I would hand myself this book and depart.

This is a very personal manual that I put together. The principles in here were acquired through regrettable mistakes. I spent many tearful days and nights as a consequence of ill-conceived ideas anchored in deep levels of foolishness. I wished someone had prepared me for this journey and said these words: "you will prevail, but the road is marred with checkpoints where you will have to make choices". This book may not offer all the answers, but the principles in here will help you to figure out the standards by which you need to abide to make these choices.

This is not a book about immigration. In fact, how you got here is not of relevance to this book. The people who were interviewed for this book came over from more than 100 countries from around the world and all of them got here through different ways and means. This book assumes that you are starting off in America with your papers in hand whatever they might be. If you do not have your papers, I am sorry for how much harder your journey is going to be. This book is going to offer very little help in that regard. My thoughts and prayers are with you and I hope you will get to a place where this book can be useful to you.

This book is not a checklist of what one must do in order to be wealthy. There are many paths to wealth. I know people who have not worked a single day in college or started a business but they are wealthier today than Babylonian royalty. I know others who carry a lot of debt by common standards, but they own so many assets that their debt seems almost insignificant. Some of the people who have contributed to this book are first-generation immigrants in America, but they come from multigenerational wealth in their country of origin and so their wealth transition to America was as simple as wire transfers. Others have coasted their way into wealth in ways that would make a Roman Empire tax collector embarrassed. Even if some of these apply to you, you will benefit from some of the principles in this book even as simple refreshers of what you are already doing.

If you have been in America for a while, have made some mistakes, and are on a journey to figure out how to turn the ship around, the principles in this book would still help. But the ones who will truly benefit from this book are those who are starting out, papers in hand. Those who want to see past the lures and traps of the system, and set themselves up for success that will be passed on to their children.

I came to America from Togo, West Africa after living in France, The Ivory Coast, Gambia, Benin and other places. I came as a college student on an F-1 visa, and before I came I applied for the Diversification Visa Program (Lottery Visa) for my mother. The results came a year and a half later: she won and our entire family was granted green cards. My journey in America is nothing but grace by which software randomly selected an unmarked envelope with our names on them. This is the reason why I have never taken my American opportunity for granted. My being in America has never been about merit or that I was better than anyone else. I was blessed with an opportunity and I was not going to squander that opportunity. And neither should you.

Unfortunately, the opportunity to live in America does not come with a playbook. You can acquaint yourself with the law and learn how not to break it; however the laws of success in America are not given to you. Many people born and raised here do not even know about the ideas and concepts in this book. I graduated college and got a job, but then I was let go and ended up living in my car for close to seven months. I was distraught. Had I left Africa to end up in America like this? How could I have squandered this opportunity and failed myself and my parents in this way? I went to school, got a degree, got a job and worked hard - but now I am sleeping in my car. How could this have happened? Where did I go wrong? After a while I promised myself I would never wake up in a car, jobless and homeless again. I prayed to God to grant me a second chance and to help me understand the fundamentals of the land I was in. I was able to get out of the car, got a job, bought a house and went on to start a couple of businesses in addition to working as a senior leader in one of the largest marketing agencies in America.

But I didn't do it all on my own. Many people came into my life and little by little they provided the structural foundation upon which my life in America ought to be built. I was introduced to the book "the Richest Man in Babylon" by George Clason, and although it was written in 1926, its laws and principles transcend time. I was later introduced to "The Way to Wealth" and "Poor Richard's Almanac" - both by Benjamin Franklin. I met people like Japheth Light who played a key role in my financial acumen development. I read "The Total Money Makeover" by Dave Ramsey and "How to Win Friends & Influence People" by Dale Carnegie. Every time I learned something new, I assessed its impact on my life and realized that had I known these things from the get go, I would have made so many different decisions. I fellowshipped with a small group which met every Sunday and they kept me accountable throughout most of the journey with a great deal of love and no regards whatsoever to my ego.

There are good and loving and generous people in America. You will meet them on your journey. Just like in other societies, there are some not-so-good characters as well. The best thing you can do for yourself, especially in your early days, is to broaden your circles as much as possible, and not just hang out with people who are of the same background as you. Expand your circles. Befriend and leave a good impression with people. Go out of your way to get to know them and enjoy the experience of learning from them and their background and their worlds. If you are of a spiritual background, anchor yourself in that life and expand your reach. If you are a Christian, find a church that welcomes outreach. If you are Muslim, do not miss Friday prayers at the mosque. If you are Buddhist, even if you do not practice, still go to the temple on open days and enjoy socializing.

My friends and I shared many horror stories of the errors we made, and although we can laugh about them now, we all agreed that someone needed to make sure other people got a chance to avoid what we did. A friend of mine who is a PhD in Chemistry kept a record of every single expense he made in college and while we were talking about this book, he shared with me how much he spent on drinks and entertainment during that time. He said "if I had invested even half of that money then, I would be sitting on a small fortune right now." Learn from him!

As you read this book, know that I am rooting for you. Welcome to America. Everything is going to be all right. Here are the fundamentals which you need to know. The rest you will figure it out. Be blessed.

01
KNOW YOURSELF

Brace yourself. It is going to be a rough ride.

The accumulation of wealth is not a pursuit in greed or a validation of ego. It is not about becoming a millionaire. Many of us are not millionaires or billionaires. Many of my friends do not wear designer clothes, drive luxury cars or live in mansions. There is nothing wrong with those, but that is not what wealth is about.

Compare two people: one lady lives in a multi-million dollar home and drives a luxury vehicle, and earns over five hundred thousand dollars a year. She however is drowning in debt and is one paycheck away from being in financial trouble. The other lady lives in a small one bedroom condo which she bought and paid for. She drives a ten-year-old used car and although she makes less than fifty thousand dollars a year she does not have any consumer debt.

It is the duty of every first-generation immigrant in America to succeed and become wealthy, paving the way for the next generation to start in a better position than the previous one. In the example above, the lady drowning in debt may be considered rich, but she is not wealthy. She might've achieved high wage earning success - but not financial freedom.

The first mistake many of us make when we get here, is to have a complex of inferiority (probably due to a language barrier, for those of us whose English is a second language) based on our origins. With this, we waste time waiting for validation from others, and we miss the fact that we already have it, simply because our backgrounds already command attention and interest. Some of us would splurge on material stuff to emulate the American life we saw in Hollywood movies or music videos. Landing on these shores legally, safe and sound is in an achievement in itself. We should not seek further validation from people whose only difference from us is that either their parents were American or their mother went into labor within the geographical boundaries of the United States. The validation you seek will be there ten or twenty years from now when you look back on what you have achieved.

The danger of seeking other people's validation early on your immigration journey is that you lose whether or not you get it. If you don't get it, you feel like a failure and quit trying to move forward. The laid back attitude that results from our perceived lack of validation and worthiness ends up costing us, in wasted time and opportunities. We settle for lower paying jobs for longer than we need to, because we don't believe that we have what it takes to earn a higher salary. We tend to lack the audacity to see ourselves as winners, or to summon the courage of a warrior. We tell ourselves that "one day" we will get there, but right now we are not there yet. For many of us, "one day" never comes - or if it does, it doesn't have the dimension of our dreams.

If you do however get the validation from your peers early on, you still lose because many of us rest on the laurels of early success and think we have arrived - when the journey has not even started yet. Oftentimes in some immigrant circles among young people, someone achieves a high-paying job early and as they start making money, they splurge wastefully. They settle on those early wins and do not invest in their future, and as a consequence, a decade later they are still in that mindset; while their peers who did not secure those early wins end up growing past them creating a better life for their families.

You need to sit down calmly and make an inventory of yourself. But first, hear me and embrace the knowledge that you are worthy of it all; go get it with all your might. This is important because you are going to be tested and your environment will be hostile at times. Solace will be found in resting on your spiritual foundation and on the belief in yourself that you are here not by mistake and that you are worthy even if the world around you does not seem to validate you.

You need to know yourself and be honest about what you know and what you don't know. If you just got here my friend, you don't know anything, and the sooner you embrace this reality and shove your ego aside, the better off you will be.

It is ok to be ignorant of some things at the beginning;

nobody is going to educate you on the concepts of American capitalism. This is something you will need to get acquainted with very rapidly. Understand how unbalanced the United States is from a macroeconomic perspective – and understand the concepts of the working class, the middle class, and the difference between the haves and the have nots. Understand the difference between being rich and being wealthy. There are a lot of rich people in America. Rich people make a lot of money; some are able to keep their riches, but some squander theirs. A wealthy person is one whose assets are greater than their liabilities. In order words, the wealthy are able to retain their riches. Your goal is to become wealthy in America, not rich.

Welcome the help of Americans, but be careful whom you ask for help. There is a big misconception in this country that everyone is where they are solely because of the choices they themselves have made. Many Americans think that if you are struggling it is somehow your own fault. Even religious people would put a spiritual spin on it: you are poor because you have sin in your life. There are many religious leaders on television who preach prosperity - defined as material wealth - as a sign of divine blessing. You will soon realize there is a lack of empathy for struggling people - never forget this! I have been blessed to be surrounded by faithful friends who prayed for me and held me accountable for my actions, but there were plenty of people who looked down on me when I was struggling.

There is a significant dichotomy between the theory of America and the reality of America, and this has always been the case. In theory, if you go to school and get a job you will be ok. In reality, there are plenty of obstacles in the way and there are a lot of educated people who are unemployed. In theory, America welcomes immigrants - and even boasts a Statue of Liberty monument which reads "give me your tired, your poor, your huddled masses yearning to breathe free," - but in reality, America blames foreigners for all their woes. In theory, the second paragraph of the 1776 Declaration of Independence reads "we hold these truths to be self-evident, that all men are created equal", but in reality it was not until the Civil Rights Act of 1964 that African Americans were considered as equal too.

Americans will never admit this, but there is a caste system that lies in the belly of the society's ethos. Unspoken yet omnipresent, a depraved morality is woven with embellished statements of patriotism. Americans will tell you that they value education but year after year, they cut the school budgets to give tax breaks for the wealthy. America loves team sports and the spirit of team and common victories but celebrate MVPs (most valuable players) to idol status.

America is therefore a great country full of hope and opportunity - but also full of complexity that you will have to navigate. To do so successfully, you need to know your strengths and your weaknesses and not lie to yourself about them.

You need to know yourself and your relationship with money. Are you a spender, or are you a saver? Do you like gadgets or do you like to spend your money on experiences like travel? You need to know yourself because the discipline required to succeed and the rewards that would encourage you when you achieve your goals need to be meaningful to you - otherwise you will fail.

You need to be clear about what money means to you emotionally and spiritually. Do you like to help people? Well, you can't help people if you are broke. How can an empty cup fill up another cup? People may say that money is the root of all evil, but wealth is obtained through the acquisition of money and its preservation. Make money, keep the money, put the money to work, and do not lose the money. It is important that you assess yourself and be clear: what makes you happy right now and what do you enjoy doing? This will help you determine what wealth means to you, and what lengths you are willing to go to get it and why. Ultimately wealth means different things to different people and you have to be clear with yourself what it means to you. How you define success will determine which actions you take for yourself as a first-generation immigrant, and what legacy you will leave for future generations.

No matter what part of the world you come from, you have heard of the importance of the company you keep. You need to be the kind of person others would benefit from being around and you need to keep good company. This is not only universally important but it will follow you throughout your entire life.

This does not mean that while you are in America you should not make friends. On the contrary, it means you should make a lot of friends, but you should be judicious of who your friends are. Part of knowing yourself includes knowing your influence on others and their influence on you. Don't underestimate the effect you can have on people. A friend of mine remembers how one of his bosses at Microsoft used to tell him all the time, "you are more influential than you think you are." You may think that nobody cares what you think but you may be surprised.

As soon as you settle into your new life in America, take as many different types of online personality tests as you can. No single test will fully explain who you are as a person, but they will give insight as to why you do the things you do and why you do them the way you do. Myers–Briggs and Truity are two of the most popular personality tests out there.

You need to devote your first few days on this journey to figuring yourself out. The good news is that you will not be the same person you are now, twenty years from now. You will change and your world view and priorities will change, but you need to fully understand who you are today and know that your fundamental motivations will not change over time. Know yourself above all. Knowing yourself will impact the career path you choose. Knowing yourself will determine what electives you choose in college; it will help you understand where you need to challenge yourself outside of your comfort zone. In fact this is how you learn to identify your comfort zone, how to grow beyond it and how to recognize when you are out of your depth.

Once you have done this work, dream: spend time dreaming and thinking about the end of the journey. When you "make it in America", what would it look like? It does not matter how crazy it looks or sounds, lean into this mental exercise because knowing yourself involves knowing what your dreams are. Lean into these dreams and set them as goals. "Shoot for the moon. Even if you miss, you'll land among the stars."

02
EARN: WORK SMART VERY HARD

Now that you have started the work of knowing yourself, you need to address the first foundation of creating wealth for yourself and the generations to come. But before you can build wealth, you need to earn, and earn a lot. People who make it would often tell you that you do not need to work hard, just work smart. They will tell you that you should prioritize balance over hard work. This is the equivalent of someone who just won an endurance race, and upon seeing you at the starting line of the same course, they tell you to go slow, take your time to enjoy the lines on the ground of the track and to not exhaust yourself. You might finish the race in good shape, but it is almost certain that you will not win first prize. Hard work is not the opposite of smart work. Smart work is incomplete unless you work hard. Smart work is manifested through the accomplishments of hard work. In the end, nobody can take away from you what you know. Knowledge is power.

America is not going to hand you anything. It is called "the land of opportunity", but not a single one of those opportunities comes to you if you are just coasting along. As a first-generation immigrant, you will have to earn a seat at the table.

As soon as you have the necessary documents to work legally in this country, work. Work for someone, work for yourself, but work and earn. The sooner you earn the shorter the distance between you and wealth. Working is the quickest way to learn about real life in America.

The establishment of wealth starts with the earning of income. Without an income, you will not be able to take care of yourself, save, invest and amass wealth. It all starts with earning. We will discuss entrepreneurship later, but before you can lead, you must learn to follow. While I was in college, I worked at a call center. That job taught me how to engage in conversation with a total stranger and get their attention. It taught me how to handle rejection and objection from others. In another job, I worked as a rep in wireless provider store. There I learned that great customer service could be turned into a strong sales funnel machine. I have also worked as a janitor at the university. That job taught me to respect the labor and the laborer no matter what the labor is and where the laborer is from. Whether you work an office job or do manual labor, excellence should be your aim. Excellence is achieved through intelligently identifying the keys to success in the job and working very hard to meet and exceed those goals. You should always show up for work with a sense of purpose, and when you clock in you remember clearly why you are there. Know where you are in the company, what the next step you are trying to achieve is and what you need to learn now in order to get there. Be an apprentice to your more experienced co-workers and ask all the questions you need to do your job well. The only stupid questions are the ones you do not ask.

A key lesson about work in this country is that Americans care about profit often above their moral standards. That is why you will see a racist business owner who would not approve of his children interacting with someone of a different race or origin, running a business that employs people of that race. He hires these people because they earn him a profit through the value of their work. Remember to be valuable. Understand what value means to the business that you work in - and be valuable. For example, if you work as a waiter, make sure that on even your worst day, you give your patrons good service. Good customer service and care make them come back and spend more and that increases the earnings of the owner of that restaurant. And that income is tied back to your employment. Creating and offering value to others around you is one of the surest ways to increase your earning potential.

You need to commit to excellence from day one. You will hear some people complain that immigrants are taking jobs away from Americans. Make it your commitment to outwork and out-excel anyone in any position you will be put. Show up first, leave last. If they ask you to go one meter, you go two. This is how you flex your "work ethic muscles". Unlike in sports, in life you don't get practice runs; every day is game day. Therefore excellence without compromise should be your aim.

Do not procrastinate or become complacent. If you are

getting paid for it, it's work. You need to make sure that you give it your very best. By pushing your performance limits even in badly paying jobs, you are learning what you are capable of. Having said that, this is not a call for blind commitment. You need to be wise in what you commit to, and learn to get out of unyielding enterprises. I recommend reading "The Dip" by Seth Godin. There, you will learn when to quit, and when to stick. This is important because you will soon learn that in most enterprises people fail because they quit the right stuff too early or they stick to the bad stuff for too long.

Whatever you do, keep a log of your success and failures. Learn from your mistakes, celebrate your wins, and then go back to hunting for more wins.

Do not conform to the standard of work ethic around you; most people are lazy and entitled. They want a great deal of reward for very little effort. Consider hard work as a barrier to entry for your future competition. Outperform your competition whether it is classmates taking the same exam, or co-workers competing for the same job/promotion. Outperform in your practice, outperform in your learning, and outperform in your execution. Be studious in school, be excellent at work, be fulfilled in your relationships. Your standards should not change because others around you are taking it easy. Work first, and have fun later. You will have a lot more fun when you are wealthy twenty years from now. Trust me, that fun will far surpass any fun you can have now that takes away from you executing your plan.

Heed this warning however my friend. Do not build a career based on something you are not naturally good at.

This is why the previous chapter is so important. Know yourself - so that when you put in the effort and you realize that you are not good at something, go seek what you are good at without losing your income stream. Do not seek happiness for there is no perfect job in itself. Seek to meet your goals, and focus on the work that gets you there.

Even if you do not go to college, these principles still apply. Higher education is a key to success in America, but education in and of itself is not what causes you to succeed. In fact, the traditional American educational system trains you to be a cog in the wheel - not to thrive in life.

Understand that you do not have room for failure. When most Americans fail, they move back in with their parents and get the opportunity to start over. If you fail, what are your options, going back to your home country? Failure is NOT an option. You did not come this far to fail, so you double up, triple up if necessary and you go the distance.

Once you have established work experience, choose to work for companies which offer equity as a part of their compensation. Whether it be stock or options, do not work for a company which does not give you part ownership. I once turned down a job at a company which offered me 310 shares (valued at $210 per share) as a part of my compensation. Seven years later that stock grant was worth close to eight hundred thousand dollars. For the sake of building wealth in America, do not work for any company that is not willing to give you equity as part of your compensation, because by doing so you are building up someone else's wealth without building up your own.

You may be wondering, do I regret that decision? I do

not. I reported to the best manager I had ever heard of or seen, and that turned out to be an invaluable experience. The decision to turn down that job was in favor of personal success and professional satisfaction. It wasn't about achieving financial success - at least not in the short term. I loved the agency I was working for and especially I put so much value in my leadership that I told myself that if I worked hard and climbed the ladder, I will make up for the money I left on the table.

I cannot pass on personal success to the next generation. The sacrifice of the current generation in favor of the next generation would have been to take the job and add eight hundred thousand dollars to my net worth and augment what I give my children one day. So remember "a good job and a good salary with the best boss" is still a good thing, if that is what matters the most to you.

03
DON'T SPEND …
DON'T GET INTO DEBT

Now that you understand the value of money and you are earning an income, you cannot spend every dollar that you earn. Spending and debt must be addressed together. Debt is the result of spending money you do not have. You get into debt because at some point you made the decision to acquire something that your current means could not afford to acquire on your own.

Several financial books and blogs on the subject of debt have found that the number one driving force behind people getting into debt is usually an egoistic desire to satisfy oneself - even if the source of satisfaction is beyond one's means. The desire to "keep up with the Joneses" or to be acknowledged by others has trapped many. My friend, forget the Joneses and live within your means. There is no lasting reward in borrowing that money you do not have in order to acquire stuff to impress others.

At its core, personal wealth is comparable to a business's equity and the formula for equity is:

Equity = Assets – Liabilities

In its more simplistic form, you have:

Wealth = Personal Assets – Personal Liabilities
Wealth = (Income+Savings+Investments+Insurance) – (Debt+Spending)

If you are willing to spend, America will equip you with all kinds of ways to spend money you do not have. Do you need a car? There are debt options for that. Do you need clothes? Every department store has a credit line they can offer you. It is a trap! Undisciplined spending will lead to unsecured debt and you will spend years making up for a gratification you were not willing to delay.

American society has always and will always bombard you with commercials and incentives to get you to spend. You have to first understand that the country needs the masses to spend and not save.

Gross Domestic Product (GDP) is the value of all finished goods and services made within a country. In 2019, 70% of America's GDP was in consumer spending. Meaning that 70% of the monetary value generated in America was generated by the retail and service industries. The combined, commercial and residential construction was only 6% of GDP. Put another way, Americans spend almost twelve times as much on goods and services than they do on their nation's infrastructure.

Do not pick up this habit. It is very hard to get rid of

even as you suffer through it. Many people have unfortunately not heeded this advice and they had to spend years correcting the mistakes that they could have avoided early on. The fundamental rule here is for you to spend less than what you make, and to not borrow in order to buy things you cannot afford.

Ask yourself if that purchase is worth 150% of whatever the sticker price is because if you are not careful that is what you can end up paying if you finance your purchases. Compound interest is the eighth wonder of the world. He who understands it, earns it ... he who doesn't ... pays it. When you finance your purchases, you pay interest on top of the original price. And if you pay slowly, that interest will compound. You want to be the one who earns interest through investing, not the one who pays interest through debts. Always consider: who am I making wealthier while I go into debt?

You may not be able to at first, but aim to get to a point where you live on less than 50% of your income, and the rest goes to savings and investing. If you commit to spending on needs not wants, focus on yourself and not on impressing others, you will find out soon enough that you will actually enjoy amassing assets instead of spending your income on expenses.

As I mentioned in the first chapter, invest in knowing yourself. Figure out who you are and be that person. Learn to improve you but be you. Do not try to live a life you cannot afford. America is really good at marketing herself, and its products to its consumers, but most folks aren't making it like bandits. Don't fall for the trap of keeping up with the Joneses. Statistically speaking, the Joneses are broke. According to an article by Megan Leonhardt published on CNBC "only 41% of Americans would be able to cover a $1,000 emergency with savings." This means that if confronted with an unplanned expense of $1,000, 59% of Americans would have to use credit cards, loans, or help from family and friends to handle the situation. As an immigrant, don't fall for the flash. Keep your pragmatic sensibilities. Labels on clothing are nothing but expensive advertising - where you are the billboard paying to advertise instead of being paid for marketing that brand.

Never buy consumer goods at full price. In America, things go on sale often; take advantage of this. There are plenty of quality products available at discounts used or unused. I personally drive a twenty-year-old Japanese import which I bought used. I have heard from many people that I should not be driving such an old car. I know for sure that one of the people who tells me this, drives a luxury European car but is drowning in debt. Remember: money talks but wealth whispers. Don't be caught up in labels, but purchase things of quality.

Over time your income will increase. Do not increase your lifestyle when your wages increase. Increase your savings instead. You would have noticed that I told you to live off of a percentage of your income (aim to ultimately live on 50%; save and invest the rest). This is important because I did not give you a dollar value. If I tell you to aim to save $1,000 dollars per month, it will seem at first impossible. My first "big" paycheck in college was $225 for two weeks of work, more if I worked overtime. A friend of mine who lives in the Midwest makes $150,000 per month. For him saving $1,000 implies that it is ok for him to waste the rest of his money.

When you have to move from one location to the next, you will have a moment of clarity. You will spend a lot of time wondering where all this junk came from. You end up throwing things away. You move to a new place and funnily enough, you buy more stuff. If you don't need it then you don't need to buy it. Here's a useful suggestion: before you make any purchase, wait 48 hours before you complete the transaction. For example you find something online, add it to your cart and go away. Come back 48 to 72 hours later and then finish the transaction. This has been a great tip for me. Usually I end up purchasing only a quarter of what was in my cart, because things that seemed essential three days earlier no longer carry the same level of attractiveness.

The other moment of contemplation for many of us is at the end of the year during tax season. You will get your W2 in the mail and it will say that you have earned some amount of money which will surprise you. This is hilarious because you know how much you are supposed to make per year, since you were told this before you started working. The shock comes from wondering "where did the money go?" The balance of your bank account more than likely does not match the numbers on your end of your tax statement whether it is a W2 or any other income statement. This moment is one of the checkpoints on the journey. The goal is to live a life in America as a first-generation immigrant in a way that when you look at your end of year summary, you don't ask yourself, where did the money go, but rather feel proud of the amount you have saved and invested. This mental shift is critical.

A friend from Guyana told me "retail therapy is a trap. You need to find alternative ways to manage your emotions. The side effects of being broke are worse than any issue you were trying to cope with."

Debt has always been a part of society's ills; the wise have warned their youth since the dawn of humanity. It is surprising how with all these warnings we don't live in a debt free world. Every culture has a warning against getting into debt and it is usually anchored around frivolous spending. You cannot get ahead by borrowing. There are a lot of financial bloggers and investors online who will claim to have tips and tricks around how to use debt in your favor - but as a rule, please stay away from debt. This is what ancient wisdom from around the world has to say about debt:

Borrowing is the mother of trouble. (Hebrew proverb)

Poverty without debt is real wealth. (African Proverb)

Debt is slavery. (African Proverb)

He who restrains his appetite avoids debt. (Chinese Proverb)

Happy is the man without sickness. Rich is the man with no debts. (Chinese Proverb)

There are plenty of ways to get ahead. The first is so basic I'm almost embarrassed to say it: spend less than you earn. (Paul Clitheroe)

Today, there are three kinds of people: the haves, the have-nots, and the have-not-paid-for-what-they-have's. (Earl Wilson)

And finally:

No man's credit is as good as his money. (E.W. Howe)

Now that we have covered the ills of credit, let's talk about the other side of the coin. Remember how I told you earlier that America is a living and breathing contradiction with itself. This too applies to debt. You cannot live and prosper in America without some sort of debt history. Notice I did not say "debt" - but "debt history". A lot of key benefits to the American financial system is axed around a metric called Credit Score.

Though it is not unique to America, its use here in this country is extreme.

A credit score is a numerical expression of the analysis of your credit files; it symbolizes your creditworthiness and is based on your credit report information collected from three major American credit bureaus.

In its primary use, banks and credit card companies use credit scores to evaluate the potential risk you pose were they to lend you money. They use your credit score to determine if you qualify for a loan, at what interest rate, and what borrowing limit should be given to you.

Credit scoring however is not limited to banks. Utility companies, cell phone companies, internet companies, insurance companies, landlords and the like, use your credit score as a proxy to determine how likely you are to pay your bills and whether or not they will provide you with services.

Some companies also use your credit score to determine your worthiness for employment. Several government departments employ the same technique.

Scores range from 300 to 850, and you have multiple credit scores from different models and bureaus and they all get considered differently. The most commonly used by all the organizations mentioned above is the FICO score. This is the one you need to really worry about. Your FICO credit score is based on five factors: payment history, credit utilization, length of credit history, new credit, and credit mix. Each factor makes up a different proportion of your credit score. You need to keep these factors in mind for the rest of your life in America, but the most important factor is payment history. The (670-739) credit score range is where the average of U.S. consumers score and it is what most lenders consider a good score.

The first time I learned about credit history, like many immigrants, I did not have any and suffered for it. There are many ways to establish credit. You can find banks which provide secured credit lines. This means you pay them $500 and they give you a credit card for $500. You use this credit card and pay your bills on time. After six months they will report your line of credit to the credit bureau. Most department stores have in-store lines of credit which you could apply for. When you are starting out, your score is going to be low so you will not have any history, so your priority is to find a way to establish credit. Be careful - some shady organizations like car dealerships will offer you in-house financing but will not report your payment history to the credit bureaus. Do your research and use legitimate means. It would not be a good thing to find out after six months that you went through all the work for no benefit.

Once you establish good credit, nurture your score. Go to the website of the three bureaus and create accounts and lock them up. Some will charge you a small fee to lock your credit but pay it. This is important to protect yourself but also to prevent anyone else from stealing your identity.

Now, you must be wondering: how do you first warn about debt, and now say nurture a credit history? The whole system works together. There is a way to combine living on half of your income, not going into debt, and nurturing your credit score. You do this through the monthly usage of a credit card. Once you have established a credit history through a secured credit card, find a rewards program credit card which offers you points for using the card but does not have annual fees, or if they do it is a nominal one. Most airlines and hotels have an entry level credit card. My recommendation is to find the airline which offers the best deals to your country of origin and get their credit card. Once you have the card, your strategy is to make sure you do not put on the card anything you cannot pay for. So that the balance of the card should be the amount of money you would have paid in cash if you were spending only cash. This is critical because most people overuse their credit cards. Do not ever put on a credit card any purchase you are not able and willing to pay cash for. This is because at the end of every billing cycle you must pay off the credit card. This means that for the rest of your life in America, the balance on your credit card at the end of the month MUST be 0. If you are not able to adhere to this discipline then keep your secured card and never use it. It is better to not have a credit score than to be in debt that you cannot pay off.

You will be bombarded by offers to get credit cards on a

daily basis. Do not get them. The "free" credit card is not free. You to have to pay it back. Every dollar you spend on debt and interest payments is a dollar you take away from your children and the next generation. If you get a credit card, avoid high interest and pay the balance off every month.

Aim to buy your car in cash, but if you must borrow to get the car, pay it off as soon as possible. Do your best to pay two or three times your car payment to accelerate the repayment period. A car is a depreciating asset, meaning that it loses value from the moment you buy it, so borrowing money to buy a car is like taking your hard-earned money and investing into an asset that loses value. We will cover houses and real estate in a later chapter.

As far as student loans are concerned many people justify it, but let me warn you, the payments are real. Even if you declare bankruptcy, student loans cannot be discharged. I have watched college students use their student loans to buy clothes and party instead of education expenses. They justified their behavior by reasoning that it was a long term debt that they do not need to worry about. Consider this factoid: former President Barack Obama took out almost forty three thousand dollars in student loans to pay his tuition at Harvard Law School. Meanwhile his wife, former First Lady Michelle Obama took out almost forty thousand dollars in loans to finance her Harvard Law education. This debt was accumulated with their undergraduate student loans which brought their total student loan debt above one hundred and twenty thousand dollars. President Obama graduated from Harvard Law School in 1991, but it was not until after he signed a multi-million dollar book deal in 2004 (the year he was elected to the U.S. Senate) that they paid off all of their student loans. A friend of mine from Barbados, who works in Silicon Valley, said this: "if you must get them, pay them off as quickly as you can, use your bonuses and tax refunds to pay them down. Don't buy other things with the school refunds but pay off the loans. I unfortunately graduated with seventy thousand dollars in student loan debt between private and federal loans. Even though I had a good job it took years to pay them off and contributed to a lot of stress." Her story is often too common. This is why you not only need to avoid student loans but you need to make sure you become wealthy enough so that your children and the next generation do not have to go bankrupt to go to college.

Stay out of debt.

04
SAVE WHAT YOU CAN... AND MORE

If you spend less than you earn, and do not borrow money to spend on things you cannot afford, you will start having money left over. These "leftovers" are the means by which you will become wealthy. Everything we spoke about up until now has been about the foundation. Here is where you start to build!

When you start making money in America, you will treat saving as what you do with what is left over, because after you pay for rent, there may not be much left. This is where I need to challenge you, my friend, to evolve your mindset and thinking!

Treat saving and investing the same way you treat your bills. In fact you must change your financial worldview as early as possible to prioritize saving as your first or second bill - depending on your religious beliefs if you have any. Most religions preach that you give an offering first. Then, your next payment ought to be to yourself. This payment to yourself includes savings, investments, and the means to develop yourself and increases your ability to earn. All personal finance gurus agree on a version of this: pay yourself first. Unless you pay yourself first, you will never stop living from paycheck to paycheck, and at the end, you will have very little - if anything at all - to pass along to the next generation.

There are two pillars to be built on the foundation of earning: saving and investing. This chapter talks about saving. Saving is not to be the only thing you do to build wealth, but it is critical. Your ability to invest is anchored on your ability to save. You cannot invest out of thin air; you invest part of what you save.

Your savings can protect you from future debt. If you do not save, you will not have a cushion to deal with life's emergencies. When - not if, but when - they happen, you will end having to go into debt to pay for them. These kinds of setbacks can wipe out any progress you may have made towards the establishment of wealth. Challenges will arise, and oftentimes they will be unexpected. Whether it is a car that breaks down and requires a lot of money to fix, or a parent dies and you need to travel to the funeral, unexpected things will happen in life and you need to prepare for them financially.

Saving for future experiences like travel makes those trips more enjoyable. I have seen people go into credit card debt in order to take a luxurious vacation, and then spend several months paying for something that they are no longer enjoying. No matter what it is that you buy or pay for, you will enjoy it more when you own it outright. Sitting on a beach in Jamaica with a rum punch in hand, sun above, sand below and surrounded by friends feels much better when the trip has already been paid for.

When you have a savings cushion you can afford to make better career decisions. I was recruited by a company I was consulting for and they wanted to give me a 20% raise above what I was making. It sounded like a lot of money at the time, but I was debt-free, I had three months of savings, and I was learning and growing a lot in my current role. Because my savings were stable and I was living on less than 85% of my income, I could continue to take advantage of the learning and growth opportunities I already had. It was easy to say no to a 20% raise – especially one that came with a toxic company with a hostile work environment. I could afford the peace of mind.

You cannot fill a cup with an empty jar. A blind person cannot lead another blind person. Saving allows you to be generous if you choose to. When you have the desire to help someone but you can't because you are broke, it hurts you twice.

Not only do you need to save, but you need to start saving very early. Whether the interest rate is high or low, you will soon understand that compound interest is your best friend. Compound interest means "interest on the interest" and is the reason why many investors are so successful. If you invest $1,000 at 2% interest, after the first year, $20 is added to your account. In the second year, your 2% interest is calculated on your entire new balance of $1,020 - not just your original $1,000. Your interest in the second year is now $20.40. Year after year it adds up. Time is your biggest asset.

Whatever you can - save. Start with what you can, but

make it a priority, and increase your saving over time.

Two friends of mine who have been married for five years, shared their budget with me for the purpose of this book.

Household Budget Allocation Worksheet	% of Gross Income
Paychecks - income: my wife and I	100%
Paycheck automatic deductions (taxes, insurance, etc.)	31%
Paycheck automatic investments (401k, etc.)	11%
Discretionary income - income under our control	**58%**
Investment and savings spending	19%
Gifts & donations	3%
Living income - After Saving, Investing and Giving	**36%**
Necessary expenses	23%
Flexible expenses - things we can live without	8%
Growth expenses - online training and other education	3%
Leftovers - to be invested in risky opportunities	2%

Notice that they live on 36% of their gross income and save/invest 42%. They save as much as they spend on themselves. Not everyone will have a two-income household, but what if I were to tell you that he is an athletic coach and she works in the retail industry? These are not glamorous jobs. This is why it is important that you do not compare yourself to others. I am sharing their budget in terms of percentages, so that you understand that it is not so much the dollar amount that you save, but rather the level of effort that you put into savings and the standard of living that you maintain for yourself. You must save at least 10% of your gross income by all means necessary. If you need to get a roommate or two to be able to afford this savings regimen, do it. You have no business living by yourself if you cannot afford to save at least 10% of your income; you are not ready for independence.

When you start a savings account, keep it separate from your main checking account, and preferably, with another banking institution. The best thing to do is to find a community bank or a credit union in your area and open your savings accounts with them. Your main checking account should be with a major national institution such as Chase, Wells Fargo or Bank of America. Credit unions are best for savings due to their low fees, ease of banking and excellent customer service, but they are oftentimes difficult to do international transfers with. If you bank with at least one of the major institutions, this will come in handy if you need to send or receive money overseas. When you get paid, transfer your savings allocation to your savings account and make sure that it is not easy to access. One of my guardrails is that I do not keep an ATM card for any of my savings accounts.

To make it easier to save, you can remove the complexity of having to make the transfer yourself. You can set up automated transfers from your checking account to your savings. Better yet, many companies offer the ability to allow direct deposits to several accounts. My current employer allows me to make deposits into up to four separate accounts. I have divided my paycheck to make sure that my savings percentage goes directly to my savings account, my investment percentage goes directly to my investment account, the household percentage goes to the household spending account, and my personal allowance percentage goes into my personal allowance account. Just like a kid in school, I give myself an allowance that is used for fun discretionary spending.

Saving has profound effects on your life and demeanor. Having savings in the bank alleviates stress and allows you to look at life with hope. Being broke is stressful. When you wake up in the morning and you do not owe anyone anything but love, and you have enough resources put away to go through six months without income, it makes the air you breathe feel fresher, the food you eat tastes better, the work you do feels lighter. It allows you to be more entrepreneurial, and it allows you to see the world around you as an opportunity rather than a problem to solve. Most people with wealth take this feeling for granted, but trust me, the first time you reach this goal, you will understand. You will love yourself and respect yourself more because you will be proud of not being broke.

05
INVEST: INTO YOURSELF
AND THE FUTURE

Simply working and saving is not going to make you wealthy in America if you do not make the money work for you. In many cultures around the world, a disciplined saver can become quite wealthy, but in a high inflation high consumerism society such as the United States of America, savings will protect you for the emergencies and the rainy days, but the acquisition and retention of wealth only happen through two strategic means: entrepreneurship and investments. Parallels can be drawn between the two.

The most important asset you have towards the establishment of your wealth is you. You are going to be the one doing the work. You are going to be the one making all the decisions which will determine if you succeed or fail. You are going to be the one that provides the elements by which people decide whether or not they should hire, partner with, or avoid you. Even in extremely conservative religious circles, where people believe that

"God is in charge of everything", a caveat is made for free will and personal accountability. So you have to embrace the role you are about to play. No matter where you come from and the journey that led you here, the journey forward is going to be hard and distractions will abound.

Before you invest though, you need to be clear about what you are investing in. You will need a plan - but not too rigid of a plan. Your life in America is going to be a negotiation between you and God (or the Universe, or Life, or Yourself depending what you believe in). The negotiation is to strike the balance between what you desire out of life (and pray for), and what you get (your current state).

So before you invest in yourself and the future, you need to know what it is that you are investing for.

I met a friend after college who changed my life. Until I met her, I had a day planner but only wrote down the things I needed to do. I did not have a system. I usually wrote things like "presentation due on Oct 3rd." She introduced me to the writing of goals, the breaking down of those goals into projects, and the breaking down of those projects into tasks to be accomplished. Later in life I was introduced to S.M.A.R.T goals.

From New Year's resolutions to dreams, people try really hard to make their aspirations a reality while actually accomplishing very little. Oftentimes, they come to realize that they were lacking the ability to clarify their ideas, focus their efforts, and use their time and resources productively. This is where S.M.A.R.T goals come in. The idea is credited to Peter Drucker's Management by Objectives concept.

The idea is to make sure that your goals are clear and reachable; each one should be:

- **S**pecific (simple, sensible, significant).
- **M**easurable (meaningful, motivating).
- **A**chievable (agreed, attainable).
- **R**elevant (reasonable, realistic and resourced, results-based).
- **T**ime bound (time-based, time limited, time/cost limited, timely, time-sensitive).

The S.M.A.R.T concept does not work well for long-term goals because it lacks flexibility, and it also stifles creativity.

So my recommendation to you is to sit down and set goals in the following manner.

- *Aspiration*
  - *Long Term Goal*
    - *Short Term Goal - S.M.A.R.T*
    - *Short Term Goal - S.M.A.R.T*
    - *Short Term Goal - S.M.A.R.T*
  - *Long Term Goal*
    - *Short Term Goal - S.M.A.R.T*
    - *Short Term Goal - S.M.A.R.T*
- *Aspiration*
  - *Long Term Goal*
    - *Short Term Goal - S.M.A.R.T*
    - *Short Term Goal - S.M.A.R.T*
  - *Long Term Goal*
    - *Short Term Goal - S.M.A.R.T*
    - *Short Term Goal - S.M.A.R.T*

For Example:

- *Graduate College and work in the Aerospace field*
  - *Graduate top of my class with Aerospace engineering degree*
    - *Get a 4.0 GPA*
    - *Win the Senior Project Competition in Aerospace*
    - *Get an Aerospace patent by the time I graduate*
  - *Get a job at a top five Aerospace Company*
    - *Get an internship at an aerospace company by my junior year*
    - *Land interviews at companies throughout college*
    - *Get a job lined up the semester before I graduate*

Earlier in this book, I encouraged you to dream. Remember the dreams that you have. The journey to wealth is a succession of set and achieved goals. You set some goals, work your ass off to achieve them and learn lessons along the way. Then you set the next one. Rinse and repeat. In between the setting and the achieving lies a lot of hard work.

In the words of the great actor Denzel Washington who rose from obscurity to bright stardom, "true desire in the heart for anything good is God's proof to you, sent beforehand, to indicate that it is yours already. Dreams without goals ...yearly goals, life goals, daily goals, monthly goals, hourly goals, minute by minute goals... Dreams without goals are just dreams. They ultimately fuel disappointment. Goals on the road to achievement cannot be achieved without discipline and consistency. Between goals and achievement are discipline and consistency."

The first investment you need to make in yourself is to get an education. Leave the liberal arts degrees to American citizens and your children - if you make it big and they choose to. There are exceptions to everything but the field of study you choose matters. By study, I do not just mean a traditional degree. If you are into carpentry or farming, you need to go to a trade school. Whatever field it is, choose wisely and get educated in that field. The good thing in America is that in the early days, you can change your major so choose your field and do extensive research on the outcome of that field. What is the average student loan debt of the latest graduating class? What is the average salary of the graduating class at graduation? What is the employment percentage? What is the average salary five and ten years after graduation?

If you are reading this book in the early 2020s, Technology is the place to be especially Machine Learning and Artificial Intelligence. Doctors and Lawyers are perennial - as every third world parent would tell you. Majoring in Mathematics is one of the most underrated and yet most transferable skill sets. Bottom line is, do your research and pick a field, but stay away from majoring in Sociology, Psychology, Philosophy, English, Business Administration (some business classes might help with your entrepreneurship endeavors, but a business degree, not so much). These are fields of study for second generation Americans.

People who know me will point out that I was a Business Administration major, but the reality is that I was an Information Systems major and added Business Administration when I realized that I could use the electives of one of the degrees as the core of the other and graduate with two degrees for the same cost during the same time length.

Whatever field of study you choose, prepare for your graduation the day you start. There are a lot of mechanics which are required in the last two years which many advisors do not tell you about, and you find out at the last minute. So you need to be informed as much as possible.

Research the top five companies in your field of study and research the top start-ups in your field of study. Next research the top three companies in your field that are close to your place of study or living (if you are studying online). Look at the types of jobs they have posted in your field on their website and start writing down your strategy.

Once that is taken care of, you need to invest in yourself as a person. In building and retaining wealth, you are your best asset. You need to be a sharpened tool at all times, or you will miss out on achieving your full potential. Earning a degree or a certificate, learning a trade, getting a real estate license, going to a financial adviser, buying and reading business books are all examples of investing in yourself. These things improve your personal, physical, intellectual, emotional, entrepreneurial, and financial acumen. Reading this book is an investment in yourself.

By reading and doing research, you will expand your knowledge and your experience. Learning about credit cards, loans and credit scores will ready you to make good decisions. Savings is how you start to build up wealth. Nobody is going to teach you wealth; so you are going to have to seek out the information for yourself in this and many other books and resources.

The first major investment in yourself, which we've already discussed throughout this chapter, is education. A formal education is important in the context of going places. Even though America idolizes those who dropped out of college to become millionaires or billionaires, most jobs or career opportunities require the presentation of a formal degree. If you can afford to go to an elite school, do it. Having Harvard and or Stanford on your resume is an undeniable advantage, but if you cannot afford it, you do not need a degree from these schools to become wealthy in this country. The smart thing to do is research the school you want to have on your resume. Research their transfer requirements. Then go to a community college which has the program necessary to transfer to the school you are aiming for. This strategy bypasses the high cost of the first two years where you are taking fundamental courses at a premium price. A friend of mine who is a brilliant chemist in Portland told me how he committed to the degree he was working on. "I did the math on what we were paying per semester, and I figured out how much we were paying per one hour class. With that number in my head, I never missed a class. If I am going to pay this much for one hour, I would reap all the benefits. So I never missed a class, and by simply sitting in a class, you are guaranteed a B. Add in a slight effort and you get an A."

Invest in yourself. Get your degree on time. Do not waste your time and resources by prolonging your college years. Failure at this level is not an option. Seek out scholarships to lighten some of the financial burdens of this stage. Keep developing your own skills to increase your investing wisdom and also to increase your earning power.

The next thing you need to invest in is educating yourself about America as a country. For this you have to really open your mind and expand your circle. Do not limit your circle of influence to other immigrants or just people you know. A friend of mine who is a savvy businessman explains it this way: "when you are in college, you are surrounded by future fashion moguls, business executives, inventors, politicians, world leaders... so you need to make as many friends during this time when you are young because these are the people who will constitute your network." As Porter Gale says: 'your network is your net worth". Hang out with people who you want to become, not just the ones you are comfortable with. This means making friends with older people who are successful; someone who can be a mentor. In fact get multiple mentors, in different fields and for different reasons. Learn from them and simply observe them. To many of us, that's the biggest thing we benefited from: going outside of our comfort zone.

If you come from a country which does not speak English, or even if you come from one that does, you need to invest in mastering and improving your communication (writing and speaking) skills. Several practical ways to do this include:

- Make friends with American citizens from different regions of the country.
- Take communication and public speaking classes as electives. Join the debate club or take part in the activities.
- Read the book "How to Win Friends and Influence People" by Dale Carnegie.

With strong communication skills will come an improved sense of self-confidence. This will be a magnet which will draw people's trust to you. Communicate well so you can set your own agenda and tell your own story.

Join a fraternity or a sports team or any kind of group dynamic that encourages not only speaking with other people but also bonding with them. Get a mentor with whom you will meet regularly.

We talked about saving in the last chapter. If you do not save, at some point in your future you will look back and wish that you started saving even $100 a month into an account when you first got here. Save until you have three months of living expenses in your savings account, then continue to save but start the companion effort of investing. There is no secret to investing. The goal is to put your money in a means that allows you to earn more money back than what you put in. Saving is a form of investing if you have a high balance on an account which has high interest rates. Again if you do not have the discipline necessary, automate, automate, automate!

We will cover real estate and entrepreneurship in later chapters, but other investment channels which you should consider early after doing your research are:

- Money market accounts which are glorified savings by which you get a higher interest rate than from regular savings. Do your research as some require minimum deposits.

- Short-term CDs (certificate of deposits) are the equivalent of a locked savings account. You put money in an account where it is locked for a period of time, often six months to one year or two years. You get your money back plus interest.

- The stock market where you buy equity in business by using a trading platform to buy outstanding shares.

- Mutual funds and index funds are good investment channels where you trade on industries and sectors rather than individual stocks.

- Bonds which are loans you make to companies and governments to fulfill their financial needs and they pay you back with interest.

- As your savings increase, consider crypto currencies and commodities (raw materials or primary agricultural products which trade on a commodity market).

- As your career advances, you may get additional opportunities such as 401k, Health Savings Accounts etc. Participate in all of these benefits. They build up over time. Always max out your 401k and other benefits. Take full advantage of the 401k match (e.g. if your employer will match up to 7%, you should do your best to maximize this benefit. It's free money!)

06
INSURE WHAT YOU HAVE AND DON'T LOSE MONEY

Imagine building a big house with everything you love inside of it. One day, a fire strikes and destroys everything. All is lost and you have no way of getting it back, because none of it was insured.

Insurance is one of the hardest things for most people to wrap their mind around. You are spending the very little money you have to prepare for something which may or may not happen. The issue is that when it does happen, it can wipe out in one moment years of hard work and sacrifice.

We don't know when we are going to die, so it is important to have things in place that take care of your loved ones were something to happen to you. Health insurance, car insurance, rental/home insurance, and life insurance are necessary for sound financial planning. That being said, be careful of equipment insurance and travel insurance. For example if you buy a $1,000 airplane ticket, it might be a good idea to insure it. However if you buy a $150 phone it may not be such a good idea because the deductible on most electronics is so high that it makes using the policy often times as expensive as getting a new phone. Do your research, evaluate what you are prone to do and are comfortable with, and then make a rational decision. Make sure that you protect yourself.

Buying things with debt is a form of losing money. The interest that you pay is money you are throwing away.

Warren Buffett is famous for his two rules of investing:
- Number 1: Never lose money.
- Number 2: Never forget rule #1.

It sounds funny but it's true.

There are no get-rich-quick schemes. For example, there are thousands of pyramid marketing schemes that surface all the time and your friends or acquaintances will try to enroll you into a program where "you will make so much money, you'll never have to work again". A pyramid scheme is a program where members attempt to make money by recruiting new participants, usually where your recruiter promises a high return in a short period of time and no genuine product or service is actually sold. If there is a product sold, the product sale is made secondary to the recruiting of members and the payment of membership fees. The primary emphasis is on recruiting new participants. All pyramid schemes eventually collapse, and most people lose their money.

According to the SEC (Securities and Exchange

Commission): "fraudsters frequently promote pyramid schemes through social media, Internet advertising, company websites, group presentations, conference calls, YouTube videos, and other means. Pyramid scheme promoters may go to great lengths to make the program look like a business, such as a legitimate multi-level marketing (MLM) program. But the fraudsters use money paid by new recruits to pay off earlier stage investors (usually recruits as well). At some point, the schemes get too big, the promoter cannot raise enough money from new investors to pay earlier investors, and people lose their money."

Do your research and be careful.

Earn and pay your taxes. The surest way to fail in America is to be on the wrong side of the IRS (the Internal Revenue Service) and not pay taxes on your income. Ignorance is not a valid excuse in the eyes of the law. Earn and pay your taxes. Pay your taxes and do not break the law.

America's judicial system is not friendly to foreigners and legal fees are expensive even if you did nothing wrong. Stay as far away from trouble as you can; you have so much to lose. If you have a green card and get into trouble with the law, you will not be able to become a citizen. Many jobs and other institutions conduct background checks before they can hire or do business with you. One moment of indiscretion, mistake or foolishness will jeopardize your ability to earn and build wealth. Even if you walk away free and clear, the thousands of dollars spent on legal fees will set you back on your financial goals. No reward is worth those risks. Don't be foolish.

As you make more money, you will be tempted to increase your standard of living. Resist this temptation. Luxury expenditures ultimately become confused as necessities. This is why it is important to set goals and revisit them periodically. If your goal was not to increase your standard of living, do not increase your standard of living. Instead as your income grows, increase your rate of saving and investing. Hip-Hop Mogul Sean "Diddy" Combs and rap legend Christopher "Biggie" Wallace said it best: "mo' money, mo' problems."

Check your credit report every year. When I was in college, a bill was sent to my old address and this oversight hurt my credit for seven years.

Be vigilant, do not lose money. Your responsibilities as a first-generation immigrant are too important for you to make stupid money mistakes. Educate yourself, be vigilant, and move forward.

07
START A BUSINESS OR TWO

Now that you have gotten here, let me break your heart. Simply earning an income, spending wisely, avoiding debt, investing and insuring your assets will not get you ahead of the game. Think of building wealth like building a house. Earning and debt avoidance are the foundation; savings, investments and insurance are the pillars and walls. However, the roof of this "wealth house" is owning a business. You see, true wealth in America is only truly achieved through owning a business. Several successful immigrants did not even go to college; instead they started businesses and have done quite well. The entrepreneur life is not for everyone, and it demands quite a bit out of you, but this is the way towards creating wealth and ultimately financial freedom for the next generation.

But before you rush off to register your first LLC, please take the time to read "The Hard Thing About Hard Things" by Ben Horowitz. This book relates the challenges that he faced in his life and during his career as founding CEO to VC at Andreessen Horowitz. It gives practical advice on how to start, grow, hire, and make the hard decisions in order to succeed. According to data from the Bureau of Labor Statistics, 20% of small businesses fail in their first year, 30% of small businesses fail in their second year, and 50% of small businesses fail after five years in business. Finally, 70% of small business owners fail in their 10th year in business.

You must realize that entrepreneurship is the road to wealth, but it is a difficult road. Not everyone who starts, will succeed. Most businesses fail. The key is to start, learn, fail, start again. Failing does not make you a failure, but you need to understand the pitfalls. You must be educated about what causes businesses to fail and what that failure looks like. If you want to build generational wealth, you must be a part of the 30% whose businesses stand the test of time beyond ten years.

Websites such as Entrepreneur.com and Inc.com, must be a part of your daily read to inspire, warn, guide and entertain you as you navigate entrepreneurship. Archived videos of TV shows such as Shark Tank will give you an idea of what you are in for. By entrepreneurship, I don't necessarily mean you must take all of your savings, go rent a building and start. There are many ways to start a business in America and you will soon learn that no matter what it is that you are selling, there is always someone who is willing to buy; you just have to find them. Remember, Americans are consumers first, patriots second.

Being an entrepreneur however is not just about making money. There is a level of respect - or "street cred" - that comes with being in the thick of running a business. Americans worship at the altar of entrepreneurship.

Though Americans admire humility, even in the most religious circles, they only recognize and reward pride. They love team sports, but reward the MVP, and glorify the status of G.O.A.T. (greatest of all time). They aspire for peace but celebrate warriors. They preach compassion but look at every exchange through the eyes of winners and losers. In the balance of the workforce, Americans consider workers the losers and business owners the winners. The very laws and fiscal policies implemented in all spheres of government (whether federal, state or local) favor businesses instead of the individual.

Another reason to consider entrepreneurship is that no matter how much you save and invest, it is very difficult to be wealthy in America without creating and selling a product or service by which you generate income. This could be done as a side business, or it could be done as a full time business, but this is one of the straighter ways to wealth. As a first-generation immigrant, your reason to start a business is so that you can pass it on to your children. When you are an employee who collects a paycheck, when you retire, you cannot pass along that job to your child.

Entrepreneurship is also important because in order to build wealth in America you need multiple sources of income, so that should something happen to one of your streams of income, the other ones will help you get ahead until you find another solution. A product or service could be as simple as delivering groceries, or tutoring in college. A friend of mine who owns a very successful tech company in Houston, TX said it best: "start early, ideally while you're still in college, work on ideas. Some will fail, but that's ok. The lessons learned will save you a lot once you find the one that works." Another friend who owns a thriving entertainment company in South Florida put it this way: "start in college or as young as possible, because even if you fail and lose everything, at this stage of your life, you still don't have anything so what did you really lose? If you lose everything in college, you lose absolutely nothing."

What makes college a great place to start your entrepreneurship journey is that you meet all kinds of people, with all kinds of ideas and needs. This is your last easy opportunity to build a diverse network. After college your network becomes more restricted. This is the time to build yourself a solid network that will help your business ventures now and in the future. I have all kinds of friends from all walks of life, and most of them go back to two places in my life: high school (Saint Lucy Foundation), and college (Florida Tech). In fact, a lot of the contributors to this book are alumni from these schools, or friends that I made through them.

Online businesses (such as software services) are good businesses to start in college because they do not interfere with your class schedules. Another friend of mine recommends tech. He chose to start a company in the software/startup space because it is one of the few avenues where experience or having capital is not required to make progress. A good idea that provides value to consumers, along with being hard working and taking steps create great return for investors.

When I was in college in the early 2000's I co-founded a radio company that played African music online. Until our company was launched, there was no place on the internet where you could stream African music. Our radio company was a huge success. To put it in perspective, Apple's iTunes

was launched two years later in 2003. We
revenue through ad streams and also promot
released records from African artists. We had D
the globe who would log into the platform in different time
zones and mix on the radio.

The promotion of this radio company is where I honed
the online marketing skills that became critical to not only
my future career but also my personal growth. Through
entrepreneurship, I developed skills that were not taught to
me through classes in college or as a part of my major.

If you sit down and look around you, you will find a
problem to solve and/or a product to sell. Find your
opportunity and give it a shot. Nowadays, there are grants
like SBIR that can award up to $1.75 million for no equity
to build your ideas. Additionally, there are venture capital
firms that exclusively focus on immigrant entrepreneurs.
Check out Unshackled Ventures & One Way Ventures.
These resources did not exist when I got started, but they
now do.

There is no good reason not to take advantage of the
opportunities that exist for entrepreneurship in this modern
American landscape.

08
OWN REAL ESTATE

Owning real estate is both a type of entrepreneurship and a type of investment worthy of its own chapter. The most finite resource on this planet is land. Real estate property is acquired and changes hands, but outside of rare cases in the Middle East where some rich caliphates have created artificial cities out of the water, Earth does not produce new land. One of the best achievements you can do for yourself and for future generations is to own as many lands and property as you can responsibly. The United States has 3.8 million mi^2 of land. That is it. The government owns some of it, and private citizens own some. Real estate is so valuable that after the great economic collapse of 2008, Wall Street firms made a run on farms in Texas and the Midwest to buy up vast expanses of land. At the end of slavery, the free slaves demanded a 40 acre land distribution per slave. A lot of economic gaps between American haves and have nots can be traced directly back to inter-generational ownership of real estate.

No matter what you do to acquire wealth, your portfolio diversification must include real estate. In fact, a real estate purchase is one of the rare purchases which can be done with debt because the property for the most part (if you play your cards right) not only retains its value but also appreciates over time. Just like entrepreneurship and compounding interest, real estate is another part of your portfolio where you need time on your side. When investing in real estate do not seek glamour. That is not the purpose. It is better to own a small house in an affluent neighborhood than to own the biggest house in a declining area. A book you must read on the topic is "Rich Dad Poor Dad: What the Rich Teach Their Kids about Money - That the Poor and Middle Class Do Not!" by Robert T. Kiyosaki.

You will learn a lot from BiggerPockets. This business has a forum, a website, and a podcast dedicated to entrepreneurship and most importantly to real estate. I wish they existed when I was in college and that I had listened to them then. Fortunes in America are made in real estate and even the fortunes made outside of real estate end up diversifying a large part of their portfolio into this sector. In 2018 Kanye West, who made his fortune in the music industry, bought a 1,400-acre ranch next to the Yellowstone National Park, and a 6,713-acre ranch in Wyoming. These purchases added to the properties he and his wife own in Miami and in Texas. A 2017 edition of The Land Report named Jeffrey Bezos, CEO of Amazon (and richest man in the world), as the country's 28th largest landowner.

Real estate investment is a long term play. So before you consider this vehicle, make sure you've already done the basics: you are earning, you have your emergency fund, you are saving, and you are investing in equities. Real Estate is

᠂ place to put your emergency funds.

There are many types of real estate investments you can make over time. Research all of them so you are ready when the time comes.

A baby step is to invest in Real Estate Investment Trusts (REITs) which are companies that own, operate, or finance income-generating real estate. They pool the capital of multiple investors, and pay out dividends. This is a baby step because it allows you to invest in real estate without having to buy, manage, or finance any properties themselves.

You can consider an online real estate investment platform such as Fundrise. This is a crowdfunding real estate model, where investors pool their money to buy multi-family units, commercial property or bundles of single-family homes. Fundrise allows non-accredited investors like you to invest with low required minimums and low fees.

Since you are already invested in the stock market, you can diversify your portfolio by inviting in real estate mutual funds and real estate ETFs. Do your research with the same level of scrutiny that you would have done for your other equity investments.

Believe or not, but simply buying a house and living in it is a real estate investment. Over time when you pay off the house, you own it outright and you can pass it on to your children or the next generation. A friend of mine, while he was in college, purchased a house and lived in it with roommates. The rents that he collected from his roommates were a form of income from his house's investment.

Another popular real estate investment strategy (made famous by many reality TV shows) is flipping – the act of buying and renovating a home in order to resell it for a profit.

You can also invest in short-term or long-term rental properties, but you must first understand the pros and cons of being a landlord for a property that do you not live in.

When your finances can allow for it, consider investing in purchasing commercial, non-residential properties, or even plots of land.

If real estate really interests you, look into obtaining a real estate license from your state, become affiliated with a brokerage firm and earn a commission by helping others buy and sell properties.

There are fundamentals to the real estate investment market which you must be familiar with - licensing, taxation, and financial implications to learn and understand - but the reward is worth it. Very few fortunes in America and abroad exist without real estate as part of their portfolio.

09
WITHOUT THE PEOPLE,
IT'S JUST AN ITINERARY

As I've said before in previous chapters, your greatest asset is you, but your second greatest asset is the people that you surround yourself with. Choose your circle carefully, but don't be a cynic. Do not judge people by their appearance or what they did to others, judge people on their actions towards you. I have been shown love by people who by society's norms would be considered morally deficient. I have been welcomed in homes and circles where I did not belong. I have been blessed by people who would have been justified to mistreat me if they chose to. I am not saying that all people are good people and that you should embrace everyone, but I am the result of many people who have poured into me. From my small group to college friends, to teachers who became mentors, to coworkers, the list goes on.

This journey we call life is about the people and there are diverse people out there. Some will disappoint you.

Disappointment and betrayal are part of life, and as you start to succeed, some would try to take advantage of you. However, the good people out there are the ones who will love you and support you no matter what. People you can travel with and have a blast regardless of where the destination is. People who are genuinely in your corner and will tell you the hard truths when you need to hear them. They will open their homes to you and give you a shoulder to cry on when you need it. Cherish these relationships.

Choose your circle carefully as guilt by association is real. If you do not want to be associated with certain behaviors, consider how closely you want to socialize with people who are known for them. Do not burn bridges but be wise.

Beware of the people in your circle who do not celebrate your successes. Entertainment mogul Sean "Diddy" Combs said it best: "pay close attention to the people who don't clap when you win". I believe in energy and that the spirit in us is fueled by what we give it, and nurtured by what we keep ourselves around. Your spirit will not thrive around people who only seem to be vocal when you fail. Still, don't let your ego have you surround yourself with "yes men" - for this will be your doom.

In all your encounters with people, make them feel special. Oftentimes people advise to make a good first impression, but let me teach you what I learned from Chris Voss (former FBI hostage negotiator): "make a good first impression, and make sure you make an even better last impression." May people's memory of you be a pleasant one. Be good company and keep good company.

Some religions require tithing, some require charity

giving, and some require sacrificing your first fruit. Whatever your spiritual prerogative is, fulfill it first. On the way to building wealth, you cannot lose yourself or your soul in the process. In old Babylon and throughout the Middle East, farmers left crops on the field after the harvest to allow the poor people to harvest the leftovers so they can provide for themselves. In Arabic, the word 'zakat' translates as 'to cleanse' or 'purification'. Basically, it means purifying your wealth by acknowledging that everything comes from and belongs to Allah. In the Christian faith, the holy book contains the question, "what good is it for someone to gain the whole world, yet forfeit their soul?" Even if you don't believe in any of these faiths, or your spirituality does not account for any of this, use some of your wealth to help others and pay it forward.

This book is not about getting rich but about building multigenerational transferable wealth. Think of the immigrant life in America as a relay race. You are the starter, and your children are the next runner to whom you will hand the baton. The effort they put into their race is anchored on how well you run yours.

As an immigrant, if your children have to go through the same struggles and face the same challenges as you did in America, you have failed. It does not matter how rich you are, what car you drive, or which neighborhood you live in. If your children or grandchildren struggle through American life as though they just came fresh off the boat, then your legacy has been one of abject failure.

If you are driving a $20K car with a car loan and your child has to take a $20K student loan to go college, it means you prioritize your enjoyment of driving a car more than setting up the future for your child. This is unacceptable. The establishment of wealth is not for you to enjoy America more as a first-generation immigrant, but rather as a way to ensure that the generation which follows you are better off than you were.

There are many immigrants who came to America and four generations later, still live in poverty. That is not ok. It is ok for Americans to be poor. It is not ok for the children of first-generation immigrants to be poor.

The system is not built for everyone to get out of poverty - and one can argue that in some cases the system oppresses the poor - but a closer look will reveal "great and mighty ones" who escape the clutches of the system. However, those "great and mighty ones" are not superheroes. The only difference between them and the rest, is that they made the sacrifice.

They decided that the welfare of future generations was more important to them than their current welfare. A sacrifice is defined as "the act of giving up something valued for the sake of something else regarded as more important and worthy".

Make time for your loved ones. It is not a good thing to leave wealth to your children or the next generation but they barely knew you. Part of your legacy is not just financial wealth but the wisdom you pass on. Make time to pour into others. Be of service to others. Do for others the things which were not done for you, even though you wished they were. In other words: pay it forward.

It is important that you look beyond yourself. You need

to start now even before you meet the people you will pass on your legacy to. Most of you reading this book are in your late teens or your early twenties, and you will probably not have children for another ten years or even fifteen years. Are you going to wait ten to fifteen years to start saving up for those children or will use this time to give yourself a ten to fifteen year head start in building something for them to have in the future?

10
SEEK WISDOM, KNOWLEDGE AND UNDERSTANDING

This book provides guidelines and examples, but no two journeys are equal or end up with the same outcome. As I have said before, you are at the center of it all. As you are reading this, I don't know what you have been through to get here nor do I know what you are capable of in order to achieve the goals you have set for yourself.

The principles in this book are timeless and universal but they do not answer all of life's questions. That is why it is important that you value learning above all. It is important that you invest in yourself - and that investment never stops.

Wisdom is defined as "the soundness of an action or decision with regard to the application of experience". The secret however, is that it does not need to be your own experience. You can become wiser by learning from other people's experiences and lives. Some of the best business lessons you will learn in America are contained in Sam Walton's biography. "Sam Walton: Made In America" is the story about the behemoth Wal-Mart. It is an in-depth lesson about grit, wisdom, and perseverance - and that book costs less than three dollars. For the price of a cup of coffee, you can acquire wisdom without having to go build a massive business yourself.

Knowledge is defined as "facts, information, and skills acquired by a person through experience or education; the theoretical or practical understanding of a subject". You are coming into a new country and a new world. It would be arrogant of you to think that you know anything about what you are about to embark on. Be confident in your intelligence and your ability to figure things out, but please be humble enough to have an open mind. Even if you know what you are looking for and how to do it, leave room for possibility. American businessman Christopher Voss said it best: "never be so sure of what you want, that you wouldn't take something better".

Understanding is defined as "the power of abstract thought or intellect"? This results in the ability to comprehend and is often manifested in sympathetic awareness or tolerance. Do not be dogmatic. Even if you are religious, recognize that you as mere mortal cannot fully comprehend the deity you worship, so be zealous for good, but humble in application.

A call to humility is not a call for false modesty. One of my favorite TV characters is from the show "Suits". Harvey Spector was often confronted for his confidence in his abilities - which bordered on arrogance at times. His response often was: "it's not bragging if it's true."

Be proud of your achievements and celebrate your wins, but make sure you take your people with you on your success journey. It will be less lonely when you are journeying with your crew.

Work hard. Practice even harder. Put in the work during the times when no one is watching, celebrate your success when that work pays off. Most people talk about overnight success because they only notice when the work is finished. The time, investment, sweat and tears are often not accounted for, but go through them with pride and with the end in mind. Do not let others tell you that your ideas are not good enough. Seek advice but remember that the advice that people give you is colored by their frame of reference and knowledge. Henry Ford the father of the automobile summarizes this sentiment best: "if I had asked people what they wanted, they would have said faster horses."

Be kind but do not let others take advantage of you. Never be embarrassed to ask for help or to ask questions.

Remember: wisdom, knowledge and understanding should be your guide and your compass.

11
IN THE END, HAVE FUN!

Many people before you have journeyed here from distant shores in the pursuit of a better life for themselves and their loved ones. You have been blessed with a great opportunity, and the fact that you are reading this book means that you take this opportunity very seriously.

Take the time to celebrate your achievements along the way and take the time to share stories with the people you are with. This book was written during the great Coronavirus (COVID-19) pandemic of 2019-2020. When January came, we all had plans for the things we were going to do and the places we were going to see. But by the time March rolled around, the world as we knew it was gone.

Many of us had regrets about the things we should have done earlier and the people we should have spoken to. There are many of expectations that come with being a first-generation immigrant in this country, and it is hard to live in America especially if you want to live with integrity.

However, if you look hard enough, the right people and the right circumstances will provide levity and comfort at all times.

In the rural areas of Benin, West Africa people build clay jars under trees and fill them up with potable water so that the sojourner traveling along the road would have a place to sit in the shade and quench their thirst. Find the rest stops in your life so you can pause and breathe in order to continue. In the pursuit of wealth do not lose yourself. Have fun because fun is contagious. By allowing yourself to enjoy the journey, you will bring joy to the hearts of those who are on the same journey as you.

Of the knowledge, wisdom and understanding you collect along the way pay it forward, to make sure those coming after you are better equipped than you ever were. That is what I am doing here.

Know that you have an immigrant brother who, just like you, came here and wondered it would all turn out. I am rooting for you. Relax; everything is going to be all right. See you on the other side.

12
FUNDAMENTAL BOOKS TO READ

Over the years, people have presented me with several books which have given me wisdom, knowledge and understanding. I wanted to share with you the books which have had the biggest impact on me. You should do your very best to read them as soon as possible.

- *The Richest Man in Babylon* - George S. Clason
- *The Way to Wealth* - Benjamin Franklin
- *Poor Richard's Almanac* - Benjamin Franklin
- *The Total Money Makeover Classic Edition: A Proven Plan for Financial Fitness* - Dave Ramsey
- *African Proverbs for the Modern Age* - Eryck Dzotsi
- *How to Win Friends & Influence People* - Dale Carnegie.
- *The Dip: A Little Book That Teaches You When to Quit* - Seth Godin
- *Think and Grow Rich* - Napoleon Hill
- *The Hard Thing About Hard Things* - Ben Horowitz
- *The 7 Habits of Highly Effective People* - Stephen Covey

- *Outliers: The Story of Success* - Malcolm Gladwell
- *The Greatest Salesman in the World* - Og Mandino
- *Rich Dad Poor Dad: What the Rich Teach Their Kids About Money That the Poor and Middle Class Do Not!* - Robert Kiyosaki
- *Sam Walton: Made in America* - Sam Walton
- *The Subtle Art of Not Giving a F*ck: A Counterintuitive Approach to Living a Good Life* - Mark Manson
- *Make Your Bed: Little Things That Can Change Your Life...And Maybe the World* – Admiral William H. McRaven
- *Crucial Conversations Tools for Talking When Stakes Are High* - Kerry Patterson, Joseph Grenny, Ron McMillan, Al Switzler
- *The Law of Success In Sixteen Lessons* - Napoleon Hill
- *The Intelligent Investor* - Benjamin Graham
- *Good to Great: Why Some Companies Make the Leap...And Others Don't* - Jim Collins
- *The 9 Steps to Financial Freedom: Practical and Spiritual Steps So You Can Stop Worrying* - Suze Orman
- *Benjamin Franklin's Book of Virtues* - Benjamin Franklin

E.K. NASSIRIM

Nasir (Arabic: ناصر Nāṣir) means "helper" or "one who gives victory". E.K Nassirim is an American citizen who immigrated from Togo, West Africa. As an ordained minister of the Universal Life Church, his ministry focuses on political studies, social sciences and personal finance matters.

E.K.'s story has been a journey of grace. He has lived with very little (once homeless and hungry) and later with very plenty (home owner, food in belly). He considers himself nothing but a sinner who has been saved by grace and given a life opportunity to do good to others. Of this blessed life, he has been given, he will give an account when it is all said and done. Recognizing how surreal and truly blessed his life is, he makes the best out of every moment he has on this earth. On his birthday every year, he gives thanks and writes his own Eulogy. He believes that writing down how he should be remembered at the end helps him to live each day with the end in mind. His Eulogy's opening lines are inspired by Steve Fry's "Let it Be Said of Us" and it reads:

"Let it be said of me that I was marked by forgiveness, I was known by my love and I delighted in meekness. I was ruled by God's peace and He was my passion. With gladness I bore every cross I was given. I fought the good fight and I finished my course."

SOURCES AND REFERENCES

www.wikipedia.com

https://www.imprintproject.org/stepstosuccess/

https://www.investopedia.com/financial-edge/0210/rules-that-warren-buffett-lives-by.aspx

Sam Walton: Made In America

Seth Godin The Dip: A Little Book That Teaches You When to Quit

https://www.cnbc.com/2020/01/21/41-percent-of-americans-would-be-able-to-cover-1000-dollar-emergency-with-savings.html

https://www.wisebread.com/chinese-proverbs-about-money-and-personal-finance

https://quotescover.com/chinese-proverb-about-debt

https://www.inspirationalstories.com/proverbs/t/african-on-debts/

https://en.wikipedia.org/wiki/Credit_score

https://www.fundera.com/blog/what-percentage-of-small-businesses-fail?

https://www.npr.org/2014/07/28/335288388/when-did-companies-become-people-excavating-the-legal-evolution

https://investorjunkie.com/real-estate/compare/

https://www.businessinsider.com/personal-finance/how-to-invest-in-real-estate-make-money

https://www.pbs.org/wnet/african-americans-many-rivers-to-cross/history/the-truth-behind-40-acres-and-a-mule/

https://www.businessinsider.com/kanye-west-kim-kardashian-real-estate-homes-ranch-photos

https://www.biggerpockets.com/

https://www.thestreet.com/how-to/invest-in-real-estate-14735368

www.inc.com

Made in the USA
Columbia, SC
15 May 2020